CONSERVATION 2000

Oceans

© Philip Neal 1993
First Published 1993

Typeset by J&L Composition Ltd,
Filey, North Yorkshire

and printed in Hong Kong

for the publishers
B.T. Batsford Ltd
4 Fitzhardinge Street
London W1H 0AH

ISBN 0 7134 6712 6

A CIP catalogue record for this book
is available from the British Library

Acknowledgements

The author and publishers would like to
thank the following for permission to
reproduce illustrations: Ardea
Photographic pages 32, 49a;
Environmental Picture Library pages 38–
9, 50–1, 58–9; FOA pages 28, 31b;
Greenpeace pages 42–3, 46–7; John
Hillelson Agency pages 30–1; Institute of
Oceanographic Sciences page 25; Frank
Lane Picture Library pages 17b, 18–19,
21, 29, 33, 34–5, 48; Network
Photographers pages 54–5, 55b; Office for
Ocean Affairs and the Law of the Sea
page 61; Popperfoto page 13; David Pratt
pages 26–7; J. Sainsbury plc page 49c;
Science Photo Library pages 10–11,
22–3; Frank Spooner Picture Library
pages 14–15, 41, 53, 57b; UNESCO pages
44, 45; UN Photographic Library page 60;
Whale and Dolphin Conservation Society
page 49b.
The diagrams on page 8, 12a, 12b, 16, 17a,
20, 24, 36, 57a were drawn by Ken Smith.
The pictures on page 6–7, 35b, 37, 40, 52,
58a were supplied by the author. The
pictures were researched by David Pratt.
Extract from *Cannery Row* reproduced by
courtesy of William Heinemann Ltd.

CONSERVATION 2000

Oceans

Philip Neal

B.T. Batsford Ltd London

CONTENTS

INTRODUCTION

The oceans of the world are vast; the whole of the land area of our planet could fit, with room to spare, into the space occupied by the Pacific Ocean alone! Yet we know relatively little about the oceans, the way they work and the life cycles of many of the creatures who live within them. What we do know is that we cannot rob the oceans, spoil them or ignore their welfare without dire consequences to mankind. The catastrophic results of over-fishing, over-pollution and sea level change are recorded in the news headlines day after day.

But there are signs that governments the world over are beginning to realise that problems cannot be left unresolved; they are starting to cooperate to protect Planet Earth's oceanic future.

The Courier (Feb. 1986), the journal of the United Nations Educational Scientific and Cultural Organization (UNESCO), put it this way:

Fuelled by the sun, the ocean is the powerhouse of the earth; the source of all life, it is a huge heat exchanger that regulates our climate, it is a source of food, minerals and energy, it offers the cheapest form of transport available to us, and, last but not least, with its restless, ever-changing beauty it seems to have been designed for the delight of mankind. . . . It is a startling fact that in many respects we know more about the moon than we do about the vast mass of water that covers over two-thirds of the surface of our planet. . . . The ocean belongs to the whole of humanity. It is the last frontier whose exploration and exploitation is the concern of all nations.

YOU are an important part of that 'humanity' – YOU have a responsibility to conserve the ocean world. Just being aware of the oceans, the problems they face and the possible solutions is the most important first step. To change your way of life in order to help remedy the ocean crisis is the second. Hopefully you will play your part; I trust this book will help, for its aim is to increase your knowledge and appreciation of the oceans.

In the morning when the sardine fleet has made a catch the purse-seiners [see page 28] waddle heavily into the bay blowing their whistles. The deep laden boats pull in against the coast where the canneries dip their tails into the bay . . . The cannery whistles scream and all over the town men and women scramble into their clothes and come running down to the Row to work . . . They come running to clean and cut and pack and cook and can the fish. The whole street rumbles and groans and screams and rattles while the silver fish pour in out of the boats and the boats rise higher in the water until they are empty. The canneries rumble and rattle and squeak until the last fish is cleaned and cut and cooked and canned and then the whistles scream again and the dripping, smelly . . . men and women, straggle out and droop their ways up the hill into the town and Cannery Row becomes itself again – quiet and magical.

This extract from *Cannery Row* by John Steinbeck was written in 1939 about the canneries in Monterey, California, USA. These canneries are no more because the sardines have long since gone from the Pacific fishing grounds where, as Steinbeck says later in the story, 'the fish ran in silvery billions'.

LET'S TAKE A DIFFERENT LOOK

**'Our planet is blue;
our planet is beautiful.'**
The words of one of the first men on the moon as he and his fellow astronaut looked back at the world they had left behind. From his new place in space it was obvious to him he came from Planet Ocean and not, as his early ancestors had called it, Planet Earth. To the travellers and map makers of the distant past the surface of the world consisted of soil and rock with a few small areas of water. The most important of these 'lakes' was at the centre of this solid mass: the 'Middle of the Land' sea they named it. We call it the Mediterranean Sea, from the Latin *medi* – middle, and *terra* – land. These early people knew that other waters existed. Their explanation was that the river Oceanus went right around the world and from it came all the other rivers and seas. In one way they were right and we, now, are wrong. At school we learn that there are five oceans when there is, in fact, only one. This ocean is separated by the continents into five parts to which map makers have given the names Pacific, Atlantic, Indian, Arctic and Antarctic.

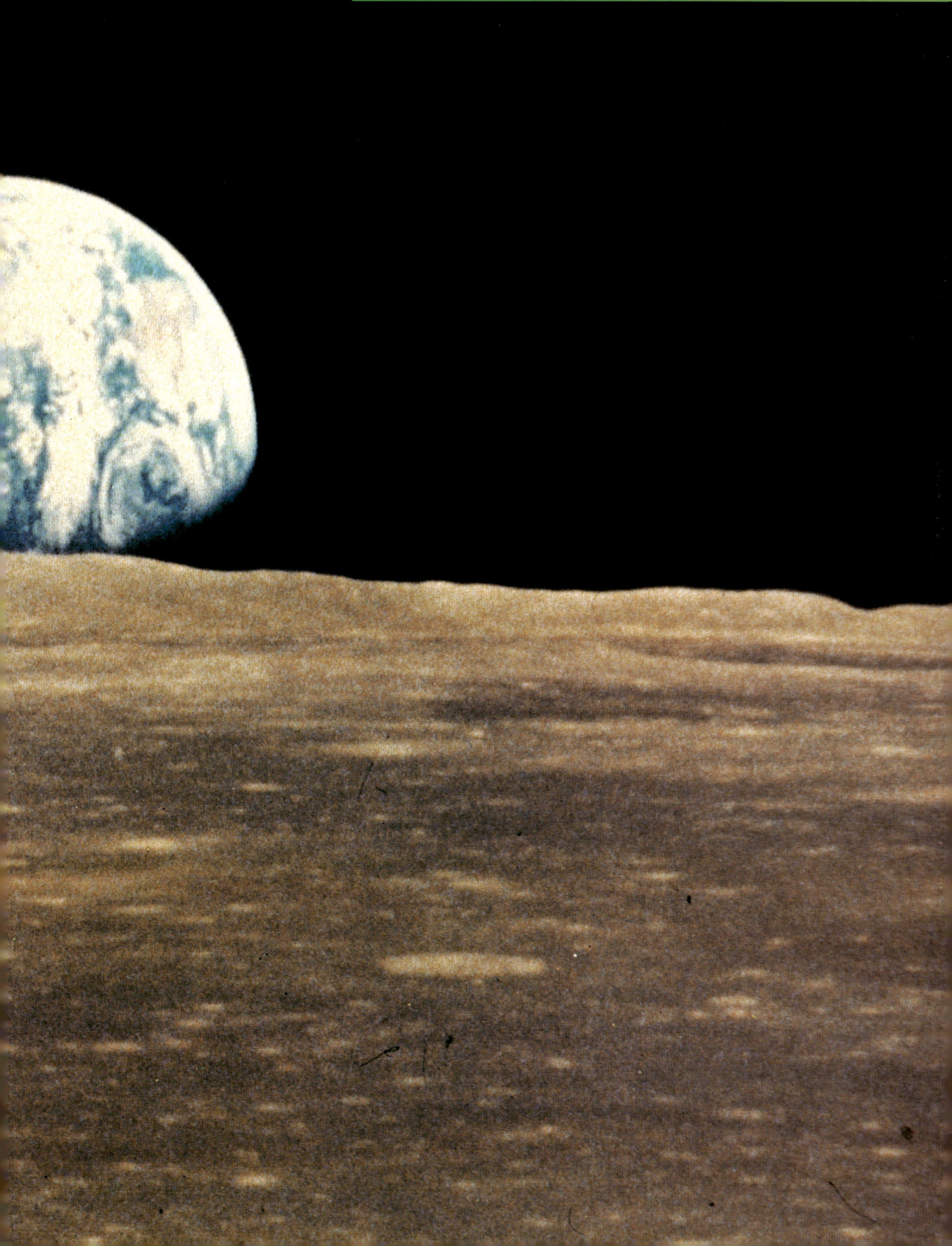

We look from the shore out at the ocean water stretching away to the horizon. We cross it by boat or plane from one land base to another: across the Atlantic from Liverpool to New York; from Heathrow to John F. Kennedy airports; across the Pacific from San Francisco to Hong Kong. We are land based and so think from land to land; if only we were to think differently we would realise that the land continents are but large islands in a single ocean of salt water. We need to take a different look.

To see the world from the ocean viewpoint is to consider our planet's environment in a different way. If we were to take this alternative, perhaps the people of Planet Earth would take more care of their precious ocean resource and stop the abuses which are so commonplace that most of us just ignore them.

Of all the planets in the solar system Earth alone seems to have rain and rivers and oceans. It is unique in having a surface temperature range which allows water to be found in its three forms of gas, liquid and solid: that is, as water vapour, water and ice.

Where and why?

Where has the water come from and why were the oceans formed? Despite the wonders of scientific discovery no one knows the answer for a certainty. One theory suggests that the water came from huge clouds around the planet which, as the earth cooled, gave up their water as rain to pour down for hundreds of years. Others believe that the

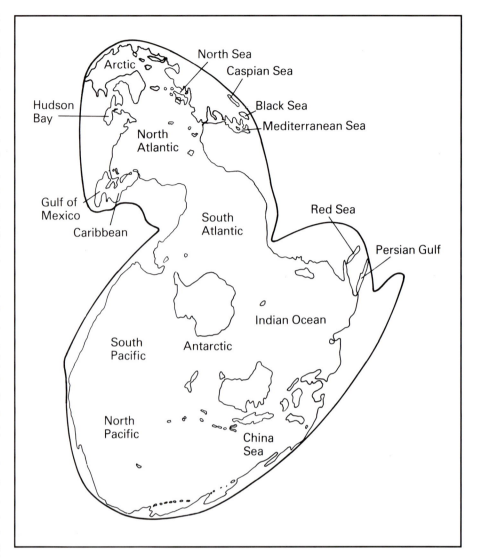

original atmosphere was wiped away during a period when the sun produced an increased heat. With no atmosphere, the water must have been generated from the earth itself. Possibly the hot molten rocks of the cooling earth released water as they began to solidify over a 1,000 million years. This released water would contain many salts and minerals making the water 'salt' as it is today. The previous idea that the rivers are constantly wearing away rocks on land and transporting their salts to the ocean would mean seawater would be increasing in saltiness. This is not so and,

It takes a photographic view from space to make the 'one ocean' idea real to most of us; it takes a clever map maker like Athelstan Spilhaus to represent Planet Ocean on a flat piece of paper. He has split the land world along a line which runs from the tip of Africa, across Asia to the Bering Straits, and continues from Alaska through North, Central and South America to Argentina. Then, as it were, he has peeled the surface from the globe and pressed it flat to show quite clearly the OCEAN as a single unit.

according to the latest theories, the saltiness of the sea has remained steady for the past 100 million years.

Oceans and seas

The enormous expanses of sea water are referred to as oceans. Parts of these oceans which are around the edge adjacent to the land coasts and partially enclosed by land are called seas – the North Sea, the Sea of Japan, the Caribbean Sea, for example. Some seas are almost completely surrounded by land – the Mediterranean Sea, the Black Sea, the Baltic Sea, and the Red Sea are of this type. Lastly there are very large areas of water fed by rivers which flow inland rather than out to the oceans. These are the inland seas, with the Caspian Sea, the Aral Sea and the Lake Chad Basin the major examples of these. Some would argue that the Great Lakes of North America, Lake Baikal in the former USSR and Lake Victoria in Africa are inland seas although they do have river connections to the oceans eventually.

The water itself

Of all the water in the world 98.8 per cent is in the ocean, over 1 per cent is trapped in the ice of the polar regions and the glaciers, while a small 0.002 per cent is to be found in rivers and lakes and an infinitesimal 0.0008 per cent in the atmosphere. The estimated volume of the water in the oceans is 1,370 million km^3 with a surface area of 361 million km^2. It achieves its greatest depth in the Mariana Trench of the Pacific – nearly 11 km (seven miles) deep. The average depth is over 3 km (two miles) (compared with the average height of the land of only 1 km (half a mile)).

The age of sea water can now be measured by the latest carbon dating system, at the same time providing evidence on the effects of climatic change. The instrument for this is at the Woods Hole Oceanographic Institution in New England, USA. The testing will help scientists chart the vast movements of water around the world and date warm periods, ice ages and sea level changes.

Sea water contains 84 of the 103 known chemical elements. Of these 57 are present in a measurable amount. By far the largest part is hydrogen and oxygen which make up 96.5 per cent. Many of the others are very valuable but are present in such small quantities that exploitation is not worthwhile; such is the case with gold. The table below shows the number of parts of the element per million parts of seawater. Only sodium chloride (common salt), magnesium and bromine are at present being extracted in significant amounts.

Table of elements in seawater

Oxygen	857,000	Iodine	0.06	Yttrium	0.0003
Hydrogen	108,000	Barium	0.03	Silver	0.0003
Chlorine	19,000	Indium	0.02	Neon	0.00014
Sodium	10,500	Zinc	0.01	Cadmium	0.00011
Magnesium	1,350	Iron	0.01	Tungsten	0.0001
Sulphur	885	Aluminium	0.01	Xenon	0.000052
Calcium	400	Molybdenum	0.01	Selenium	0.00009
Potassium	380	Nickel	0.0054	Germanium	0.00007
Bromine	65	Tin	0.003	Chromium	0.00005
Carbon	28	Copper	0.003	Thorium	0.00005
Strontium	8.1	Arsenic	0.003	Scandium	0.00004
Boron	4.6	Uranium	0.003	Lead	0.00003
Silicon	3.0	Vanadium	0.002	Mercury	0.00003
Fluorine	1.3	Manganese	0.002	Gallium	0.00003
Argon	0.6	Krypton	0.0025	Bismuth	0.000017
Nitrogen	0.5	Titanium	0.001	Lanthanum	0.000012
Lithium	0.18	Cobalt	0.00027	Gold	0.000011
Rubidium	0.12	Cesium	0.0005	Thallium	0.00001
Phosphorus	0.07	Cerium	0.0004	Helium	0.0000069

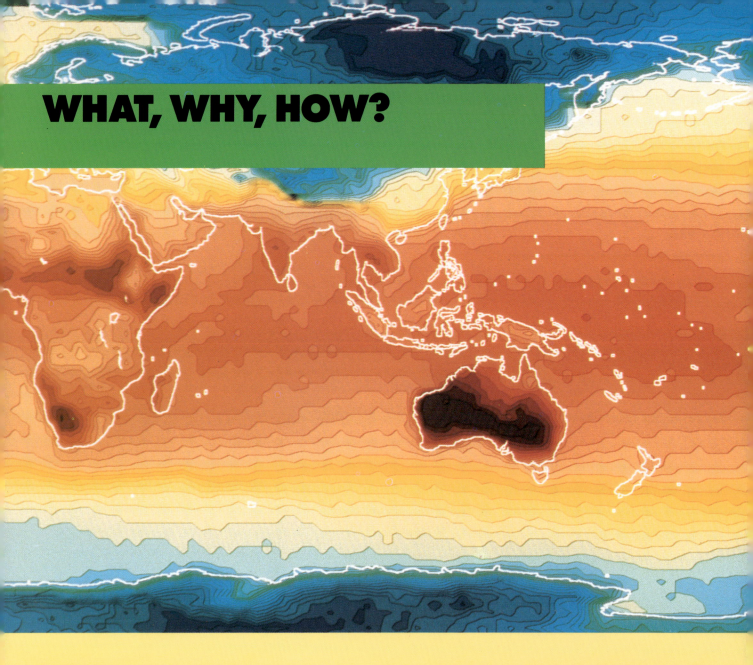

Tremendous volumes of water rotate like giant whirlpools, clockwise in the oceans of the northern hemisphere and anti-clockwise in those of the south. Their movement is stimulated by the reaction between atmosphere and ocean surface – the sun's heat, the friction force of the wind and the spinning of the world on its axis provide the power needed for this to happen.

As it spins the earth also revolves around the sun with the equatorial regions receiving the most direct heat. Thus the waters of these areas are warmer than those to the north or south. The temperatures shown on the map were those in January 1979 when it was summer in the southern hemisphere. The bluer the colour the colder it is and the redder the colour the warmer it is – black is the hottest. Most of the world surface temperature is shown to be dominated by the hot ocean areas around the equator.

Heat expands the water which raises its level enough to create a surface 'slope', 'downhill' towards the poles. At the polar regions the water is cooler so that it contracts to make it denser than that at the tropics. (Every litre of cold water is heavier than a litre of warm water.) The polar cold water sinks beneath the approaching warm water and slowly spreads back to the equator along the ocean bed.

These global movements are

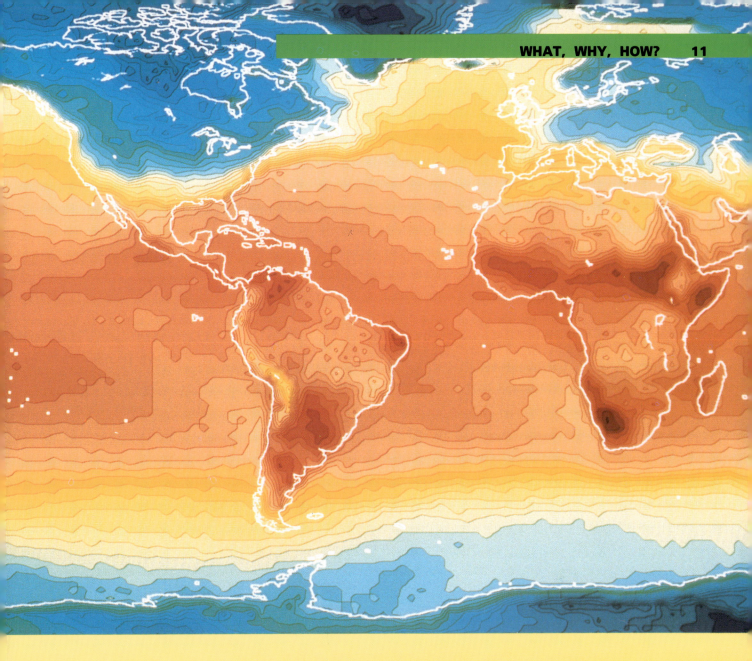

the ocean currents which act, as it were, as ocean rivers. The Gulf Stream Drift of the North Atlantic Ocean, can be observed up to 80 km wide, about half a km deep and moving about 4,000 million tonnes of water every minute of the day and night. It clearly affects the ocean temperature off the British Isles in the top right corner of the map.

A satellite map of the world's average surface temperature in January 1979. The colours represent temperatures from the coolest: mauve and blue = −38 to −12°C; to the hottest: red and black = 36 to 40°C.

The tides

The regular rise and fall of the water of the oceans is known as the tide. It is caused by the gravitational pull of the moon and, to a lesser extent, the sun. (Although the sun is bigger than the moon, it is much farther away.)

When the moon and the sun are in line, at the time of the full moon and the new moon, the pull is the greatest and the tides are the highest: these are the **spring tides**. When the moon and the sun are at right angles to each other (the quarter moons) they are pulling against each other so that the total force on the ocean is less. These high tides are lower than the others and are known as the **neap tides**.

In the majority of places high tides occur twice a day at intervals of 12 hours 25 minutes; they

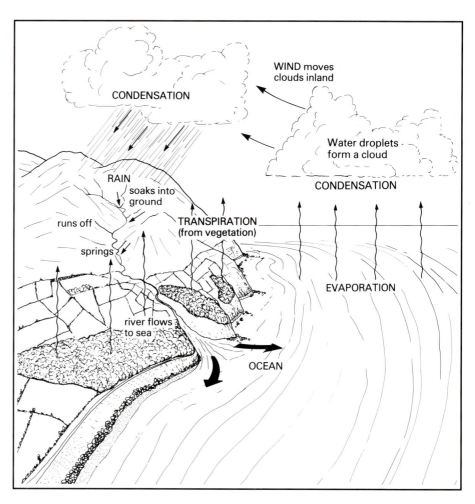

The diagram above represents in a simplified form the way water is evaporated from liquid to water vapour (gas) and rises into the air. Here it condenses back into liquid as water drops to be moved by the wind over land to fall as rain (or sleet, hail or snow). In a variety of ways it moves back into the sea or evaporates directly into the air – the water cycle is complete.

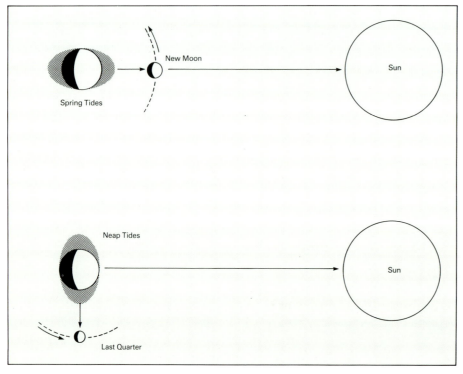

Diagram (left) showing the spring and neap tides.

Kon Tiki, an Inca-type balsa log craft, commanded by Thor Heyerdahl, drifted from South America to Polynesia in 1947, to prove that wind and currents could transport simple people-carrying boats across vast oceans.

are called 'semi-diurnal' tides. Once-a-day (diurnal) tides occur in some places – the Alaskan coast of the USA for instance. In others the position of an obstruction, such as a large island, permits the high tide to approach by two routes. The time delay involved causes the high tide to reach its peak, start to fall, then to rise again. This is known as a double tide.

For the adjacent land the critical factor is the highest level the water will reach; this will determine the extent of any flooding. If winds blow onto the shore at the time of high tide the fall of the tide may be delayed. If, at the same time, snow begins to melt, or excessive rain is pouring extra water into the river estuaries, the result will be flood conditions. This is a factor to be considered where global warming is affecting sea levels.

The waves

The surface of the ocean is disturbed by the wind which sets up ripples which we call waves. These appear to move the water forward whereas it actually just moves up or down as the ripple passes through it. Look at a seagull sitting on the sea – as the wave passes it goes up and then comes down, but it stays in the same place. At the shore, or if the wind is ferocious and blows the water off the top of the wave, the wave will break to give the white foaming water we all know well. The distance from the place where the wave starts to where it finishes is known as the 'fetch'. The further the fetch the larger the wave, providing the wind keeps blowing strongly. As a result, shores on the edge of wide oceans, such as the Californian coast of the USA or the western coast of the British Isles, have the largest waves. This is where the surfboard riders find the best waves for their sport.

Coasts

The junction between the land and the sea is known as the coastline and the area over which the sea moves, where sometimes it is dry land and sometimes under water, is the shore. The slope of the land and the type of rock exposed determine the nature of the coastal area. Where rocks are hard and resistant to the pounding from the waves, cliffs are formed. Most hard rock areas have beaches which are made of pebbles and rock pools at low tide. Softer rocks break down more easily so that the coast is covered with mud or sand often backed by sand dunes. The vegetation which grows locally enhances the coast so that, for example, mangrove trees give a different type of shoreline from that of the tough marram grasses. Warm waters encourage animal growth, the ultimate example of which is the coral polyp whose way of life gives rise to the coral rocks so common around the islands of the Pacific Ocean. It is important to recognize that shore areas vary. As a result, oil spills, for instance, will have far worse consequences with one type than with another.

NORMAL AND
ABNORMAL CONDITIONS

The world of nature is complex and forever changing but, by and large, it follows a series of patterns to which life on earth is adapted. To take one example: the seasons in the temperate latitudes cause daily variations in weather, but they follow the overall pattern of events well known to people and to nature. From spring through to late summer, trees grow leaves, flowers and fruit, after which the branches become bare, to sprout again three or four months later. Birds, beasts and all the other wildlife also follow an annual pattern of living. Though the 'normal' may be varied and may have modest alterations from one year to the next, life is able to cope with such differences.

The 'normal' is, among other things, conditioned by the 'normal' behaviour of the ocean with its temperature, tides, currents and the rest of its general pattern of existence. It is when things change dramatically that the 'abnormal' conditions take over, with consequences which may be disastrous to people and to the natural world. A gradual rise in sea level, for example, may bring about sensational results in time of storm to low-lying, highly-populated areas, such as the Ganges delta. The repeated floodings have caused severe disruption to agriculture and heavy loss of life in Bangladesh.

Temperature control

The currents transfer warmth around the world so that places which are the same distance from the pole can have major climatic differences. Take the Labrador coast of North America and compare it with the western shores of Europe. While the estuary of the St Lawrence River is frozen solid, the waters of the Bay of Biscay and the English Channel are ice free during the winter; yet they are on similar latitudes. This results from the warming effect of the Gulf Stream Drift. (See the ocean temperature map on pages 10–11.)

The oceans have an even greater influence on world climates than that directly arising from warm or cold currents. Water heats more slowly than the land but retains its higher temperature longer as the land nearby cools during winter. The water temperature variation is much less so that it has a moderating influence on land and atmosphere. This means that the oceans of the world are an important brake on global warming – to be discussed later. It is this variation in the speed of heating which is the primary trigger for the monsoon winds of South-East Asia. The land/sea temperature differences between seasons causes a reversal of wind direction. The winds which blow on to the land carry moisture-laden air from the Indian and Pacific Oceans to give the rainy season – the monsoon rains essential to farming in Asia.

Coriolis effect

The spin of the earth deflects any moving object, be it tennis ball, inter-continental ballistic missile in flight, wind or ocean current. Deflection is to the right, north of the equator, and to the left in the south. This is known as the Coriolis Effect (named after the Frenchman Gaspard Gustave de Coriolis who first described it).

The Ekman Flow and the Sargasso Sea

Inland seas are one thing – an 'in-ocean' sea is another. In effect this is what occurs in the middle of the North Atlantic, which is occupied by a large area of water known as the Sargasso Sea. Whereas the Caspian Sea is surrounded by land, the Sargasso is surrounded by major ocean currents. The swirl of the North Equatorial Current, the Gulf Stream Drift and the Canary Current encircle it.

This area of ocean is different in several ways. It is the result of interaction between the winds, the Coriolis Effect and the friction of the surface layer of water with that below. The combined forces cause the Coriolis Effect to be so great that the resulting movement of surface water is at right angles to the direction of the wind. This is known as the **Ekman Flow**. In the North Atlantic the winds are mainly from the west in the north and from the east in the south. The result is that the Ekman Flow of water is from south to north from the equator and from north

The monsoon effect, where dry winds blow from land to sea in January and wet winds blow from sea to land in July, is triggered by the varying temperatures of the land and sea. The diagram shows the normal cycle of events. If the Greenhouse Effect increases the temperature over the ocean by only a few degrees, the whole process may be disrupted, resulting in the failure of the monsoon rains, which in turn would cause a failure of crops – particularly rice.

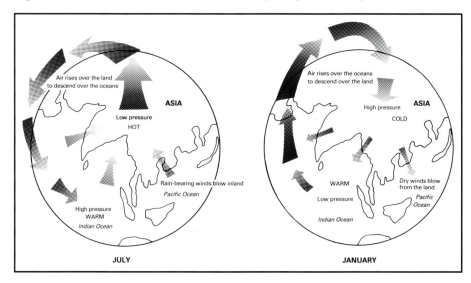

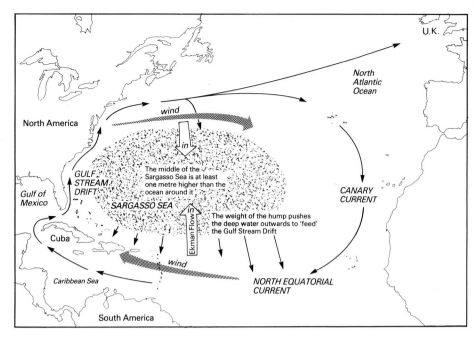

The Sargasso Sea.
This is a large area of ocean in the North Atlantic around Bermuda and the Tropic of Cancer, covering at least 5,000,000 km² (2,000,000 square miles). The surface warm water flows towards the centre; the deep cold water flows outwards.

These gigantic waves, photographed during a hurricane in the 1940s, are just one example of the abnormal weather conditions resulting from the El Niño effect.

to south from the polar area: this causes the water of the central North Atlantic to hump up so much that the middle of the hump is over a metre higher than the edges: this is the Sargasso Sea. The weight of water at the centre pushes outwards to feed the Gulf Stream Drift.

El Niño – an abnormal condition

Off the coast of Peru in South America a cold current of water normally washes against the shore. But, every so often, about once in five or six years, the equatorial current moving west across the Pacific Ocean, reverses its direction to create a tongue of warm water 13,000 km (8,000 miles) long. It takes little imagination to realise that this will change the

'normal' conditions. The weather becomes 'abnormal' giving rise to hurricane force winds and causing major disruption to the world's largest weather system, that of the tropical regions. As a result, when El Niño, as it is called, is at its worst, drought will occur in some places, while others will

suffer flooding. Starvation and homelessness follow from this. Why call it El Niño? In Spanish it means 'the child' and the conditions of change occur about Christmas time, the time of the coming of the Christ Child. El Niño is a name appropriate to the season.

Marine creatures can be grouped according to which level of the sea they inhabit. Those near the surface are called pelagic, those that live deeper are demersal and the ones which live on the sea-bed are known as benthic.

Plankton

The basis for the existence of almost all marine life are the plants and animals collectively called **plankton**, which float near the surface. The **phytoplankton**, like their plant cousins on land, absorb carbon dioxide and emit oxygen. They provide, as it were, ocean grass on which myriads of small animals, the **zooplankton**, graze. Fish and other marine animals feed on the zooplankton, while larger fish and other creatures feed on them in turn. This is the food chain of the ocean.

Coccolithophores are part of the microscopic phytoplankton. Spread over the ocean surface they are known as 'blooms', covering vast areas of over 400,000 km² (150,000 square miles). Although they are algae, they have the remarkable ability to form skeletons of chalk (calcium carbonate). These protective shells reflect sunlight back into space, which, along with the carbon dioxide they absorb, is an important factor in controlling the Greenhouse Effect (see pages 52–3).

Krill are part of the zooplankton. They are similar to shrimps and eat both animal and vegetable food. They themselves are food for sea birds, crabs, squid, seals and, almost unbelievably, the baleen or blue whale. They exist in Antarctic waters in huge numbers – one estimate suggests they weigh in total between 300 million and 6,500 million tonnes. Although krill are abundant they are beginning to be hunted by trawlers from many countries, especially the former USSR, Japan and Chile, so that overfishing is a definite possibility. Krill are eaten as paste, shrimps, krill sticks or just added to other foods to give them a 'seafood' flavour. The chemical industry also uses krill extracts to make dyes, fabrics, cosmetics, adhesives, drugs and paper strengtheners.

Cetacea

The group of mammals which includes whales, dolphins, porpoises and narwhals are called Cetacea. The minke, right,

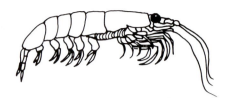

Krill, drawn here to actual size, live crowded in such swarms that the sea appears to be pink. They feed by filtering small plants and animals from the rest of the plankton using the bristles which cover their legs.

bowhead, fin and blue are all types of baleen whale. Instead of teeth in their mouths they have bony filters called 'baleens', rather like large hair combs. They take in huge gulps of the top layer of sea water containing plankton, which they force out through the baleens, keeping the food inside the mouth. The other types of whale are flesh eaters – their mouths contain teeth with which they eat fish, seals and smaller cetacea.

Cephalopoda

Octopus, squid, nautiloids and cuttle-fish each have tentacles coming from a distinct head. The first two are hunted as food, particularly by eastern and southern tropical countries of the world. Squid is popular in Mediterranean countries and can be found on the fishmongers' slabs of the USA and the UK. It is particularly plentiful in the Antarctic Ocean at the present time but, despite attempts at controls, countries are overfishing the area.

Fish

Of the large creatures in the oceans, fish are the most common, ranging in size from large sharks and rays to small sardines. Almost every variety has a fascinating life history, from salmon which spawn in fresh water but live most of their life at sea, to flat fish which inhabit the ocean bed. These begin their lives as 'normal-looking' round fish but as they grow, the young change to a flat shape with one eye 'travelling' around the body so that both eyes finish close together, looking up from the bottom.

Coelenterata

This group includes corals, jellyfish and sea anemones. These, too, have fascinating life stories. The corals, for example, build rocky homes for themselves which give rise to the coral reefs which form important natural features along tropical coasts. Mining, tourism, trawl fishing and sea-level change are environmental hazards to the future well-being of coral areas.

Most jellyfish move around by pumping water out of their bodies like a jet engine, but one type, with attractive names such as the Portuguese-Man-Of-War or the Jack Sail-By-The-Wind, uses air filled 'sails' to be driven around the oceans at the whim of the wind. Sea anemones are so named because they look like flowers, but they are animals, anchored to the rocks, preying on passing small creatures.

Crustacea

Crabs and lobsters and other hard-backed creatures scavenge the sea for their food. In some places pollution is having such a devastating effect on crabs and lobsters that they are in danger of disappearing altogether from some well-known areas. Shrimps and prawns are equally vulnerable.

Mollusca

Cockles, whelks, oysters, mussels and clams are but some of the shellfish which are used for seafood. With other molluscs it is the attractive shell which has commercial value. As all of these creatures feed on the detritus (bits and pieces) which fall to the bottom of the sea, they are badly affected by pollution. They can absorb poisons which are then passed on to people who eat them; untreated sewage pollution is particularly hazardous.

Life at great depth

In 1977 the US mini-submarine *Alvin* explored the seas two-and-a-half km (one-and-a-half miles) deep off the Galapagos Islands in the Pacific Ocean – the islands made famous by Charles Darwin. The scientists found water as hot as 17°C (64°F) heavily impregnated with hydrogen sulphide which is normally poisonous to animal life. Certain

bacteria are immune to this poison and provide the food for larger creatures. Thus, in these abyssal depths they found giant tube worms, clams, snails and sulphur-coloured mussels.

Marine life can be said to include sea birds: some, like the penguin, actually live for much of their life in the water, while others, from the albatross to the puffin, feed on fish. Pollution and overfishing seriously affect bird numbers, so much so, that they are often the first sign of something being wrong with the ocean area where they live and breed. A strong sea bird population is an indication of a 'healthy' sea.

DAVY JONES' LOCKER

Why bother with the sea-bed? Apart from making sure the depth of water is sufficient for ships to sail safely is there any point to undersea exploration? Curiosity, even if there were no other reasons, is important: who knows what may be discovered of benefit to humankind?

Where the ocean is fairly shallow, in the areas immediately close to the land, examination of the sea-bed is relatively easy. Snorkelling and Scuba (self c-tained underwater breathing apparatus) diving are popular with holiday makers, especially over the wonders of a coral reef. The Scuba system is also used extensively for near-shore investigation by professional divers.

Only in the recent past has it been possible to produce a detailed map of the ocean bed. You can see on this map how islands are just the above-sea-level part of individual undersea mountains or mountain ranges.

The most important exploration has to be carried out using deep sea technology which relies on manned and unmanned apparatus.

Topographic relief map of the world's ocean floor, showing underwater trenches, ridges and mountain ranges.

Commercial exploitation

Apart from scientific investigation, the main motive for exploration is commercial. Oil wells are now common in ocean areas such as in the Gulf of Mexico, and the Persian Gulf, or off the African coast and under the North Sea. Oil and gas are extracted by drilling into the sea-bed. Less common is the 'mining' of rare and expensive metals – gold, cobalt and manganese for example – which occur on the ocean bottom. The sea-bed also provides a base over which pipe lines and cables carry international communications, power and resources. Tunnels through the bed rock are routeways for underwater travel.

How is this exploration and exploitation carried out? Early seamen assumed that the oceans were bottomless with powerful gods and fantastic creatures inhabiting mysterious kingdoms. Sailors, drowned at sea, joined them in what English-speaking crews called 'Davy Jones' locker'. What lies beneath the surface has always intrigued explorers. Aristotle, in the fourth century BC, wrote of diving cauldrons and snorkels in order to allow people to investigate underwater. Leonardo da Vinci, 500 years ago, drew plans for underwater devices. Diving bells were actually in use in the sixteenth and seventeenth centuries; water-tight barrels a hundred years later were followed by submarines and hard-hat diving suits in the last century. The 1943 invention of the aqualung by Jacques-Yves Cousteau and Emile Gagnan made it possible for 'ordinary' people to explore under the ocean surface down to a depth of 45 metres (50 yards).

It was the laying of the trans-Atlantic cable in the 1850s which stimulated sea-bed mapping. The first detailed map of the North Atlantic was produced using information gathered with a sounding line weighed down with a lump of lead. In 1912 the loss of the new passenger liner *Titanic* prompted the use of echo-sounding devices, which led on to all the sonar (sound) instruments used now. Multibeam echo systems were introduced in the 1960s. These allowed wide areas of the sea-bed to be mapped rather than just a single line. New views of the ocean bottom landscape could now be reproduced to rival those drawn for the dry land surface.

The use of space satellites has resulted in very accurate measurements being made of the shape of the ocean surface itself. Perhaps surprisingly, it is not 'flat', as the gravitational pull of features on the bottom causes ups and downs on the surface. With satellite altimeters such as Seasat and Geosat, it has been possible to measure these to within an accuracy of three to six centimetres. Since the surface reflects the bottom shape, new seamounts (undersea hills), ridges, valleys and rifts have been discovered. The new charts produced are vital for use by the new submarines and submersible craft whose

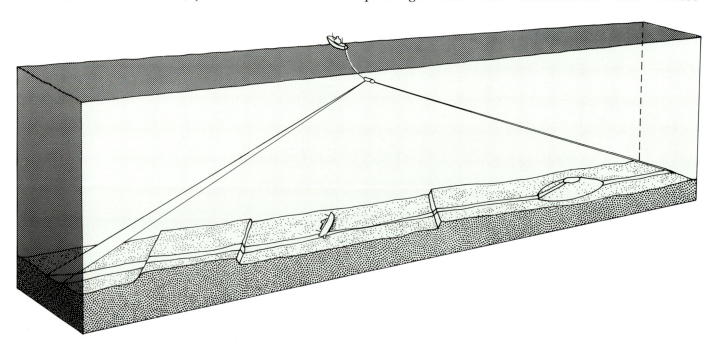

crews investigate marine life and mineral resources. Yet, despite all this activity, the ocean-covered world is so vast that less than two per cent of it has been investigated. Space has been called the 'final frontier', but this is not true while the ocean deep remains a mystery.

Ocean bed resources

It was the recognition that valuable resources are to be found at depth which stimulated modern exploration and exploitation (collecting them for use). Natural gas is one such resource, but the most important so far must be oil. Oil well accidents made headlines as with the 1980 Ixtoc 1 oil rig in the Gulf of Mexico. There, after 295 days of escaping oil, 600 million litres (134 million gallons) remained in the sea to pollute the nearby coasts. In the North Sea the 1988 Piper Alpha disaster made world news with the deaths of 167 workmen.

It is now the turn of metals and minerals to receive attention. The technology exists to lift or suck mineral deposits from the ocean bed, although such techniques are so expensive that their use is not yet worth while. Manganese nodules about the size of large potatoes litter the floor of many parts of the ocean, particularly areas of the Pacific, Indian and Antarctic. As well as manganese they contain iron and other metals. Mineral-rich muds are found in areas of volcanic activity, such as off the Red Sea coasts. Gold is to be found in the sediments off Alaska, New Zealand and Australia. Marine polymetallic sulphides (MPS) are mineral-rich deposits solidly attached to the rocks of the ocean bed. Cobalt is to be found as bread-like crusts adhering to the bottom rocks.

Environmental damage resulting from undersea mining

- The extraction of minerals and metallic ores will disturb the sea bottom and its animals and plants.
- Any unwanted waste will spread as a plume and 'drown' the ocean bed.
- Disturbing the bottom will muddy the water and stop light reaching living things.
- Clouded water will prevent predators spotting their prey and, likewise, prevent the prey seeing the predator.
- Any chemicals, poisons or other waste which has settled into the bottom sediment will be disturbed to affect life in the area.

Unfortunately experience has shown that it will be economic factors which determine whether or not undersea mineral extraction takes place, not environmental issues. The extraction of any mineral will depend on whether it is more or less expensive than mining it on land or whether it is in short supply on land.

One big question is 'Who owns the ocean bottom?'

Gloria (Geological Long Range Inclined Asdic) (*left and far left*), is a device towed behind a research vessel which uses long-range sidescan echo sounding (sonar) to build up a picture of the ocean bed. An area the size of Israel or South Korea can be surveyed in a day.

USES – FOOD SUPPLY

The oceans and seas of the world have throughout history supplied an important yield of food, particularly to island and coastal dwellers. As preservation methods improved so people living far away from any seashore have had the benefit of the harvest of the sea. Fish and shellfish have been the mainstay of the ocean food trade. Although larger mammals, such as whales, have made a contribution, in general it has been such species of fish as the cod, herring and haddock, together with crabs, clams, cockles and other crustacea, which have dominated catches. But the catching has been no more than hunting, one of the most primitive and indiscriminate forms of food gathering. Little concern has been given to managing the ocean wealth in the way that any normal farmer would manage the fields and forests. Now warnings of mismanagement are common as species of fish once abundant have become more difficult to find and many of the traditional fishing fleets of the world are lying idle in their ports. Methods of hunting, overfishing and polluting of breeding and living areas have, as we shall see later, brought about this critical situation.

The ocean as a direct source of food is overwhelmingly important for humans, but there are other uses for marine life. Fish oils are part of the cosmetic, drug and industrial trade; fish meal is an important fertilizer for agriculture; extracts, such as iodine from seaweed, are used for medicines; shells, pearls, and corals form part of the jewellery or ornament business.

A fishmonger's slab shows fish, shellfish, cephalopods, mammals and reptiles. Each will require a different method of catching depending almost entirely on where they live in the sea – near the shore or far out to sea, near the sea-bed, at the top or in between. Traps, such as lobster pots, are needed for certain creatures such as crabs, eels and lobsters. Lines with baited hooks are used to catch many varieties of fish, particularly from boats fishing in-shore. Squid and octopus are caught by line and so too are very large fish such as shark, although that is mainly for 'sport' fishing. Most fish, however, are caught with the use of nets.

Let us take a closer look at the way some of these creatures are caught.

Demersal trawl

The demersal trawl is one which is dragged along the sea-bed by two cables attached to the trawl boat. The net is like an enormous string shopping bag with a wide, open front end and a closed narrow tail or 'cod-end'. Rollers on the bottom of the net disturb the fish which then rise and are enveloped by the net. Small fish escape through the larger spaces between the ropes which make up the net itself, called the mesh. At the tail of the net the mesh is much closer so that the fish are trapped. After being dragged along for a time the net is hauled in and lifted by winches so that it dangles above the boat deck. A

Korean fishermen hauling in a purse seine net. The sea birds show that there are fish in the net.

retaining rope at the cod end is undone and the catch spews out onto the deck. Unwanted creatures, usually dead, are thrown overboard, while the rest are often gutted before being boxed in ice.

Mid-water trawls operate in a similar way, but floating free in the upper water.

Seine net

Catching fish with a seine net is common practice for pelagic fish, those which live in the upper parts of the sea. The net is much wider than a trawl net with a cable attached to each side. One cable is fixed to a floating buoy and the other to the boat which sails in a semi-circular course back towards the buoy.

A purse seine is a huge net with a rope around the top. When the purse 'string' is drawn tight the fish are trapped inside. The net is pulled towards the boat and fish pumps, like giant vacuum cleaners, suck the whole catch into the holds.

Drift net

Drift nets, nowadays made of almost invisible nylon filament, hang like tennis nets just below the ocean surface. They may be attached at one end to a boat, between two boats, tethered to buoys or just allowed to float free. Those that float free are proving to be a particular menace to marine life (see page 48).

Farming the sea

Aquaculture is the process of farming in water. This has always been common practice on land. In China, for example, flooded fields for rice are stocked with fish as an extra 'crop'. In Britain eels are reared in the warm water discharged from a nuclear power station. Fish farming in sea water has been less common until recently, although oysters, crayfish, crabs and lobsters have been 'encouraged' to grow in a number of places.

Salmon farms use floating cages in sea inlets stocked with salmon, while crayfish farms are to be found in river locations. Unfortunately some American crayfish imported into Britain were infected with disease which has now spread to local crayfish and has resulted in the death of whole colonies.

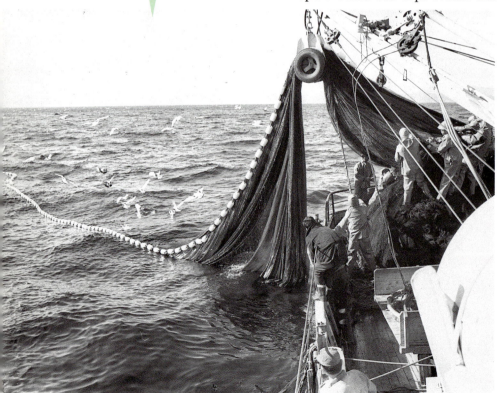

A fish farm in Norway. Salmon are propagated artificially, and grown inside large enclosures.

Shrimp farms along the coast of Ecuador have replaced mangrove swamps where all sorts of marine life used to spawn. Breeding shrimps for the farms are hard to find so that the problems of continuing to produce farmed shrimps are now very serious indeed.

Plant farming is also possible in the sea, akin to arable farming on land. Seaweed, particularly a type called kelp, is grown commercially in Japan and other Far Eastern countries to provide food, alginates used in cosmetics, food and medicine, and iodine for pharmacy.

Medicine from the ocean

Marine life provides drugs and other pharmaceutical products. For instance, slime eels from the Pacific provide heart stimulants; the tissue of box fish can be turned into a local anaesthetic, and corals contain substances which can affect the efficient functioning of heart and blood vessels. As with the rainforests, it is very important that humankind does not destroy something which may contain substances of great value but which, as yet, have not been discovered.

Fact Tunny are kept in large retaining nets in Japan's inshore sea areas. They are fed until large enough for slaughter.

Fiction? Two schemes are under consideration:
● Ocean cowboys to round up large fish in order to drive them into pens
● Whale farms to reduce the need to capture wild whales (the plan to rear whales includes the idea of collecting whale milk!)

The adverse effects of salmon fishing

● Farmed salmon escape and breed with wild salmon. The result may be a type of fish unsuited to the rigours of migration across the ocean and a later return to spawn in rivers.
● Food pellets and fish droppings fall from the farm cages to the sea-bed. The over-rich stimulation of algae causes deoxygenation of the water.
● Chemicals such as Nuvan spread, killing parasites and destroying the larvae of crabs and lobsters.
● Diseased fish may be put into the cages by mistake. In Norway, for example, some imported salmon were infected with the Helminth parasite which is reckoned to have spread into 20 salmon-spawning rivers. The only way to eliminate the infection was to poison the rivers to kill the parasite. Inevitably other wildlife was killed, including wild salmon.
● The killing of predators is carried out by fish farmers who naturally do not wish to lose their 'crop' to herons and seals. It has been estimated that over 1,000 seals, 200 herons and 2,000 cormorants or shags are killed by North Sea farmers annually.

USES – TOURISM AND TRAVEL

The increase in the availability of different kinds of fairly cheap transport in the Western world has made it possible for ordinary people to travel. Going to the seaside at home or abroad is no longer reserved for the well-off. Package holidays, which take advantage of inexpensive charter aircraft and modern hotel blocks, are the basis for an enormous holiday industry – the colourful brochures and TV holiday programmes entice ordinary folk to spend at least one part of their year 'on the beach'. All around the world, even those parts which a few years ago were unknown to the holiday traveller, are now mass tourism resorts. The quaint fishing villages have turned into bustling copies of similar 'package' places the world over. Hastily erected hotel and apartment blocks have been allowed to spread along the coastline spilling onto the very beaches which people have come to enjoy. Haphazard developments in the popular destinations of the Mediterranean and Caribbean have been followed by the exploitation of the more distant destinations of South-East Asia, East and West Africa and the islands of the Indian, Atlantic and Pacific Oceans.

These shells have been dredged up from the ocean bed to sell to tourists in gift shops.

Yet the enormous population explosion at peak periods in seaside towns brings with it environmental problems and, to a lesser extent, cruise and trans-ocean liners contribute to global pollution.

Social upheavals have affected the whole life of the local inhabitants of popular holiday centres. Tourism is an important source of income and much better conditions have resulted for some of those who work in the hotel and leisure trade. But for others, their whole life style has been upset by the regular 'invasion' of foreigners with money to spend. The pleasure-making of the visitors is not always peaceful and in accord with local traditions of good conduct.

The effects on the marine environment

In many cases the whole coastal ecosystem (the complete natural world of plants and creatures in one place) has been upset if not completely destroyed. Some of the most interesting natural shores of the tropical world are backed by mangrove trees: these are the ones whose roots are uncovered at low tide and around which a whole fascinating group of animals live – mud skippers for example. Although they are fish they are able to live for a time in the air on the mud. Other shores are the home of the coral polyp. Over thousands of years coral reefs have accumulated to attract the fabulous varieties of colourful tropical creatures and

plants which we see in television travel documentaries. Warm sandy beaches may be the nesting ground for turtles. The sight of these animals lumbering up the beach to excavate a nesting hole, lay a clutch of rubbery eggs, cover them and return to the sea is only matched by the sight of the infant turtles emerging from the nests and rushing helter-skelter for the sea before predatory foxes, birds or other enemies gulp down a tasty meal. Barbecues on the beach, noise and light from coaches and cars and turtle spotting, discourage the natural cycle of events even if the actual beach nursery has not been destroyed by building developments.

Sewage and garbage are the result of the seasonal population explosions. Much of it is discharged into the sea through outfall pipes some of which do not even cross the beach itself. As we shall see later, animal life is destroyed, algal contamination is encouraged and the beach itself is blemished by unhygienic and

Mangrove swamps are common along tropical coasts and the estuaries of rivers. They provide a breeding ground for millions of creatures. Unfortunately they are indiscriminately removed to make tourism possible with hotel developments and beach facilities. Other activities, including shrimp farming, cause the mangrove to be destroyed.

unpleasant effluents. Cruise ships and trans-ocean liners, while offering the traveller the benefits of luxury living, also pollute the seas.

Tributyltin oxide (TBT)

The sea is an inviting venue for sporting activities of all sorts. Motor vessels contaminate the water with their engine and other discharges. Sailing boats may seem to be less polluting but a recent development of modern science has had a disastrous effect. One of the problems with boats is that certain sea creatures mistake them for rocks and try to make their home on the underwater hull. In particular, a species of shellfish known as barnacles attach themselves very firmly indeed. These encrustations can become so thick that they actually

The breeding cycles of creatures such as this green turtle, can be seriously disrupted by the ever-increasing numbers of tourists in once remote areas.

Attracting tourists – a cautionary tale

Tourist development without proper planning can lead to disaster. The citizens of Dumaguete City on the island of Negros in the Philippines, decided to lengthen their airport runway so that bigger jets could bring in more tourists to enjoy the clear warm sea water and the beaches of golden sand. The lengthened runway jutted out into the sea like a long pier. A few months later the hotel owners noticed that huge wedges of sand were being gouged out of their beaches by the sea. Marine specialists discovered that the extended runway had altered the flow of tidal currents in the bay – no one had consulted them at the planning stage. The currents now scoured the beaches removing the sand and clouding the water. A hasty wall was built to protect the beach hotels so that they would not be washed away themselves. Now with sparse beaches, dirty water and an unattractive sea wall few tourists come at all to Dumaguete City.

(As described by Don Hinrichsen in his book, *Our Common Seas*.)

prevent the boat from moving smoothly through the water. With large ships it may be no more than an inconvenience, but with yachts, where going as fast as possible is part of the fun, it is essential to keep the hull clean. Scraping barnacles from the hull is one routine matter of yacht maintenance, but a modern treatment has been to paint the hull with tributyltin oxide (TBT). This chemical compound kills the larvae of the barnacle and other shellfish and so prevents them attaching themselves to the boat. It works well – but it also kills off harmless larvae and in particular those which people want, such as oysters, cockles and whelks. TBT has been banned from use in many parts of the world on inshore boats as these are the most lethal to creatures breeding near to the coast.

Transport

Trans-ocean transport remains the prime method of moving heavy goods around the world. Nothing has a greater impact on the welfare of the oceans than the bulk transport of oil and natural gas. Such movement is highlighted in later pages. Canals across narrow strips of land separating one ocean from another may have helped travel but they can have adverse environmental effects. The Suez Canal enables a connection to be made to avoid long distance sailing around the cape of South Africa. This cut between the Red Sea and the Mediterranean has meant that both seas have become heavily used waterways with the consequential contamination of both areas. The Panama Canal links the Atlantic with the Pacific obviating a long journey around South America in the fierce seas off Tierra del Fuego.

USES – POWER

Waves pound the shore during times of storm, destroying cliffs, hurling huge rocks and shifting pebbles and sand along the shore. The power of this water movement is intense and anyone who has attempted to sea bathe when the water is only mildly rough will know the pressure and force it exerts. The rise and fall of the tide is regular and forceful. If the energy in wave and tide could be harnessed it could provide a source of unlimited 'environmentally friendly' power production.

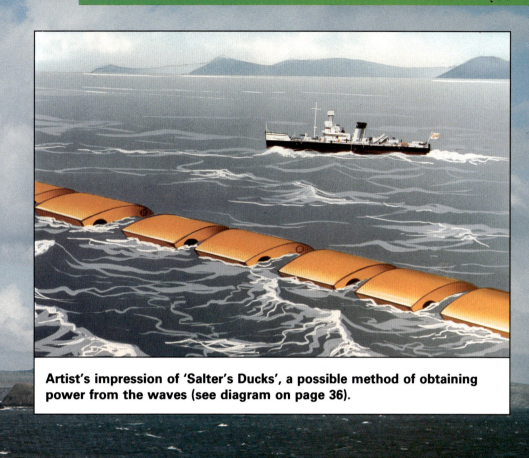

Artist's impression of 'Salter's Ducks', a possible method of obtaining power from the waves (see diagram on page 36).

Using the tides

Falling river water can be made to move water wheels which then turn machinery, usually grain-grinding stones. Similarly, high-tide water can be trapped behind a barrage until the level on the other side sinks as the tide falls. The high-tide water can now be released to fall onto a wheel. Tide mills were common enough near to the coast. In England 32 are known to have existed in Devon and Cornwall and one at Wood-bridge, in Suffolk, was still operating until a few years ago having been used for at least 800 years. With high tides about every 13 hours it meant that these mills were working at different times each day – not popular with millers and customers.

Stored high-tide water can be used to turn the turbines of electricity power stations. In river estuaries the rising water is restricted in the narrowing river entrance and the height of the water becomes greater than the same tide along the coast nearby. If the high tide is held in the river when it has reached its highest point it can be released later to turn the turbines.

Six tidal power stations are working around the world: three in China and one each in Canada, the former USSR and France. The Canadian example has been constructed in the Bay of Fundy. If the first experimental station is successful an eight km long (five miles) dam will be built across the whole bay. Over 100 turbines will be used and up to 4,800 megawatts of electricity generated. Fundy has the largest tidal range in the world with the water rising up to 16 metres, higher than a five-storey building! The second highest is in England's River Severn where a tidal barrage has been planned for years. It could be made to generate about five per cent of all the electricity needed in the UK every year. Unfortunately tidal barrages interfere with the movement of boats and migrating fish such as salmon and eels. Marshland used by birds would be drowned and riverside holiday resorts affected. Yet a road across the barrage would link one side with the other.

Tidal races are places where the flow of water is restricted between two pieces of land, for example, between two islands. The rising tide rushes through and could be harnessed to generate power.

Using the waves

The oceans are restless and only on the most exceptional days are there no waves. Although it appears waves move water forward it is only moving up and down, except when the wave breaks on the shore. If this movement could be 'captured' it would be possible to use it to generate electricity. Several ideas have been proposed, but all of them have the problem of getting the electricity generated from the sea to the land where the power is needed. Floating objects on the sea could be a hazard to boats, with some of the waves bouncing off installations making the sea rougher for small craft. Even fish shoals might be disturbed by the power equipment. On the positive side, lines of 'wave' machines might protect the shore from

Open coast barrages

Along coasts where the tidal range is high it would be possible to build a barrage to enclose a large area of the sea (rather like an enclosed harbour). In it the rising tide could be trapped to be released through turbines. This scheme would not have the disadvantages of river estuary tidal barrages. In addition wind turbines could be erected on the barrage away from the land where they can be unsightly.

Attempts are being made to harness the energy of the ocean waves. One such method has been devised by the British inventor Stephen Salter. A succession of vanes or 'ducks' are linked to a central spine by a rotary pump which, in turn, operates a generator. As the ducks bob up and down, each part is made to move. To produce the amount of power made by a 2,000 megawatt power station would require a line of ducks 400 km (250 miles) long.

erosion and many maintenance jobs would be created. One type of wave-power scheme not only makes electricity but takes the salt out of sea water to provide fresh-water supplies.

Another system is known as Tapchan (TAPping the CHANnel). Waves move down a narrow channel in the coast to fill a reservoir. The trapped water is then released via turbines to produce power. The basic idea is similar to a hydro electric power station on a river. A Tapchan plant has been operating since 1985, near Bergen in Norway producing about 350 kilowatts of electricity. Tapchans could be built to produce 300 megawatts, a sizeable contribution to any power supply.

Using the heat of the ocean

Ocean thermal energy conversion plant (OTEC)

The surface of the ocean absorbs heat from the sun, making the top layers of water warmer than the bottom. If the warm water is used to evaporate a chemical, ammonia for example, the gas given off can turn a turbine. Cool water from the ocean deep can be pumped up to cool the ammonia gas back into liquid for further use. An OTEC is working off the coast of Hawaii.

Deep ocean water cooling

Water can be drawn from the ocean deep to cool the steam used in a conventional power station on shore, turning it back to water. Though not direct ocean power it does contribute to increased efficiency. Such a station in Hawaii saves nearly £250,000 ($500,000) a year by doing this.

In the Oscillating Water Column (OWC), waves rise in a cylinder so that air is forced out of the top, turning a turbine. As the water falls again, it also operates a turbine. The Toftestallen OWC in Norway has been producing an average of 500 kilowatts of electricity per year for many years.

Using differences in saltiness

Where rivers join the sea there is both salt and fresh water. Through a chemical process called osmosis this difference can be used to generate power. Electricity is already being made in the Dead Sea area of Israel using salinity gradients: that is, the difference in the salt content of the water.

Using ocean currents

The Gulf Stream moves at a steady rate of just over three knots (the measure of speed at sea). It is only an idea at present but it might be possible to suspend turbines in the moving current in order to generate electricity.

Waste slag from the steel works – take it out to sea and
DUMP IT

Raw sewage from the seaside towns – pump it out to sea and
DUMP IT

Sewage sludge from the treatment works – put it in a barge, take it out to sea and
DUMP IT

Rubbish on board ship – tip over the side into the sea and
DUMP IT

Dredge the silt from the dock bottom – take it out to sea and
DUMP IT

Waste water from the nuclear power station – pump it out to sea and
DUMP IT

Rock debris from the coal mines – take it out to sea and
DUMP IT

Unwanted munition (arms, high explosive and gas) – take it out to sea and
DUMP IT

Waste oil in the ship's tanks – wash it out into the sea and
DUMP IT

Toxic chemical waste – seal it in drums, take it out to sea and
DUMP IT

Gut the fish in the factory ship – throw the offal into the sea and
DUMP IT

Mine the metals from the sea bed – separate out the sediment and
DUMP IT

Nuclear waste from the reprocessing plant – seal it in glass, take it out to sea and
DUMP IT

Effluent from the factory – pour it into the river which flows into the sea and
DUMP IT

The ocean myth

The ocean is vast; the ocean is deep – too deep to matter: sea water will destroy the poisons; it's cheap to chuck things in the sea; it's easy to chuck things in the sea; under the water – out of sight.

Just one great garbage dump – one mighty trash can – dump it in the ocean – who cares?

WE SHOULD CARE – ALL OF US. The trouble is most of us see little of what is happening. On land we see the rubbish being collected – we often see the trucks dropping their loads of trash into huge holes in the ground – landfill disposal. We see litter blowing around our streets. But even if we see the ocean regularly, it is unusual to see the outfall pipes or the tanker vessels out at sea dumping every kind of rubbish. Around the coast the high tides leave litter on the tide lines. We can identify plastic bottles, fishing net, plastic beer-can holders, wood and all the other debris left by holiday-makers on the beach to be washed along the shore by the waves (it's called longshore drift). Sometimes the unhappy sight of an oiled seabird or a seal strangled by one plastic ring of a six-pack holder or a sea bather with a badly cut foot will bring home to us just a fraction of the damage and suffering which is being brought about by dumping at sea.

Of the material artificially dumped at sea 80 per cent is sediment dredged from river and harbour bottoms. It consists of clay, sand and silt, together with the sewage and wastes of former times. Of the other 20 per cent of waste dumped into the ocean the most part consists of domestic and factory rubbish, much of which could have been recycled, plus sewage. In the industrial waste there are chemicals, metals and oil.

How is it dumped?

Waste reaches the sea in one of several ways:

- via outfall pipes
- discharge into a river and so on into the sea
- deliberately dumped from ships
- accidental discharge – this applies mostly to oil.

The ash and cinders left over after waste has been burnt on land is often taken with other solid waste in the dumping ships. As it falls down to the sea bottom chemicals within this material may poison marine creatures. The solid debris will settle on the sea-bed and smother the benthic (bottom living) life. It will interfere with the breeding cycle of fish. Pheromones are the scents given off by one creature to attract a similar creature of the opposite sex – smothering by dumping will interfere with this process. Food, too, will be covered.

It is true that most deliberate dumping is into the deepest parts of the ocean, where it is anticipated least damage will be done, but navigational errors lead to such well-planned operations going astray. The dumping of unwanted weaponry has traditionally taken place at sea, from scuttling ships to heaving canisters of poison gas over the side. Drums of gas dumped in the North Sea after the Second World War have been found on beaches in a dangerous condition – how many others have released their deadly cargo by now?

Progress has been made by

Pieces of rope, wooden boxes, line and hooks all 'escape' from fishing boats: most of the time this is accidental but a nuisance nonetheless. Marine creatures become entangled in pieces of net. Fine filament drift netting is the worst, although the heavier trawl netting causes suffering as well. It is a common sight on the timber of breakwaters.

Detergent chemicals are used to break up oil slicks like this one in Alaska, causing the oil to fall to the ocean bed and destroying most of the marine life beneath. Booms, like a row of sausages floating on the water, surround oil spills to prevent them spreading or entering harbours or bays. Oil skimmers are like giant vacuum cleaners which skim the water surface and take away the top layers containing the oil. Oil is retained on board and clean water is returned to the sea.

international agreement to ban or reduce dumping at sea as we shall see on the final pages. Before the introduction of plastic containers and packaging, this was not too serious a problem. Most rubbish would have bio-degraded – in other words, it would rot away in time. But most plastic (and glass) remains in its original state for as long as can be foreseen. Much of it floats so that it spreads around the world at the whim of the wind, tide or current. Discarded or lost fishing nets drift about as well, snaring marine life and causing suffering and death.

Oil

By far the most publicized dumping is that of oil pollution. The 1991 Gulf War focused world attention on the dangers of oil spilled into the sea. The release of oil into the sea was used as an offensive Iraqi tactic to impede the landing craft of the Coalition moving troops into Kuwait, and also to contaminate the desalination plants providing fresh water for the local population. This deliberate pollution was preceded by the accidental discharge of 50 million litres (11 million gallons) of oil by the oil tanker *Exxon Valdez* on 24 March 1989. The giant tanker was heading for the open ocean from the Alaskan oil terminal of Valdez, when it hit a reef, damaging its starboard oil tanks and running aground. Over 260 km² (100 square miles) of sea and shore were polluted, with the fear that the Alaskan current might carry some of the oil into the North Pacific Ocean. In the end it was the local Alaskan area which suffered most, especially the wildlife such as seals, sea otters, salmon, herring and many other species of mammal and fish. No one will ever know the exact number of dead creatures.

Despite these two examples of major incidents it is still the 'normal' deliberate outwash of waste oil from tankers and diesel-engined ships which accounts for most of the pollution. Some oil is also spilt or leaked from pipes at coastal refineries. With strict controls some ports have achieved a very good record of non-pollution – but it costs money!

Nuclear waste

Waste from the nuclear industry is divided into low, intermediate and high levels. Low-level waste is dumped at sea, but less now than before. The USA, for example, stopped nuclear dumping in 1970. Britain still discharges liquid into the Irish Sea from the Sellafield nuclear plant in Cumbria. Sweden buries nuclear waste under the Baltic Sea, while Britain and Japan are investigating this method of disposal. Turning waste into glass blocks (vitrification) before deep-ocean burial is an alternative way of dumping despite the fact that any radioactive leakage will be spread by ocean currents. For more on the nuclear problem see *Radiation and Nuclear Energy* in this series of books.

ABUSES – SEWAGE AND CHEMICALS

Sixty per cent of the world's population lives within 100 km (60 miles) of the sea. This represents about 3,500 million people who produce approximately 700 million tonnes of solid human waste every year. Much of it goes directly into the sea as raw, untreated sewage. Some is partially treated before disposal into the sea. A small proportion is fully treated with only the solid sludge being deposited in the ocean. The effect is varied, but always objectionable – it is medically dangerous and visually unpleasant.

If the neighbourhood near to the sea is industrial then the sewage will contain chemical and metallic waste from the manufacturing processes. Factories with riverside locations will discharge their effluent into the water for it to be taken downstream to the river estuary and out to the sea. The air will be washed clean by the rain falling through the fumes blown from the factory chimneys.

The gases and particles will react chemically with the water and also end up in the sea. The very thin layer on top of the water – called the **Lipid Microlayer** – will become toxic (poisonous). It is in this layer that the plankton food for sea birds lives – the deadly consequences are obvious.

If everything were dumped into the ocean deep perhaps it would not matter. Unfortunately most waste finds its way into areas fairly near to the shore – the continental shelf is the region most abused by humankind. Dead sea birds, ulcerated fish and un-well seals are but some of the signs that parts of the oceans cannot cope with the poison and sewage poured into them.

Toxic discharges

It is possible to identify poison-ous chemicals poured into the seas all around the world. Some-times these poisons reach disast-rous levels and the source can be identified. In one infamous case the Chisso chemical factory dis-charged methyl mercury into Japan's Minimata Bay. This was absorbed by fish and shellfish later eaten by the local people. Between 1953 and 1960 fish died, cats 'danced' in the streets, people twitched and their legs and arms twisted. Blindness or death en-sued. Babies were born deformed.

Yet it was many years before the connection was made between the marine pollution and the Minimata disease. At the Sandoz chemical works in Basle, Switzer-land, there was no mystery. On 1 November 1986 a huge fire was put out by the fire brigade smoth-ering it with water. This water ran off into the Rhine carrying with it 30 tonnes of herbicides, pesti-cides and mercury. Fish and eels were killed in their thousands and drinking water supplies were

Copacabana, in Brazil, is one of the most famous holiday beaches of the world. Less attractive are the effluent discharges from the city of Rio de Janeiro behind it, seen clearly in this photograph.

All is not increasingly bad. Scenes like this, of the River Seine in Paris, taken in 1966, used to be a common sight. Now detergent foam and other waste products are no longer the major problem that they were.

poisoned. No one knows what damage was done when the 50 km (30 mile) long poison slick reached the North Sea.

Some chemical waste is not destroyed quickly by sea water, but remains a danger to marine life for years. PCBs, DDT and dioxin are particularly nasty. Polychlorinated biphenyls (PCBs) are widely used in the electrical industry. If they reach the sea they are absorbed by plankton which is consumed by small creatures and, eventually, by larger animals, some to be consumed by people. Creatures die, while in humans PCBs cause cancer.

DichloroDiphenolTrichloroethane (DDT) is an organochloride made up of hydrogen, carbon and chlorine. DDT is a powerful pesticide now banned in many countries. It persists for years, passing up the food chain and settling in body fat. It is even found in the blubber of Antarctic penguins. Of the one-and-a-half million tonnes of DDT made before 1970, one million is estimated to lie within sea-bed sediments. If these are disturbed it will return to the food chain. Yet DDT has rid many areas of the world of the malaria-carrying mosquito.

Dioxin is another very poisonous chemical produced in manufacturing processes. It escapes into the air, eventually to be washed out by rain into the lipid microlayer to accumulate in the ocean food chain.

Sewage disposal

Human waste is known as sewage and in the developed world it is mostly flushed away in lavatories and treated at water purification works with the remaining solid waste disposed of by various means. In a few places, such as China, the waste is put in biogas converters for its ultimate use as a source of fuel gas and fertilizer.

In coastal areas raw sewage is often poured into the sea and this includes the USA and UK. On the coast of West Africa raw sewage from about 50 million people is pumped directly into the coastal waters. Lagos, Nigeria deposits about 13 million gallons (60 million litres) into its coastal lagoons every year. The seas near New York, San Francisco, Athens, Barcelona, Sydney and

London are some of the areas polluted with sewage.

The bacteria in sewage can cause illnesses such as typhoid and hepatitis. The nitrates and phosphates in sewage stimulate the growth of seaweed and phytoplankton. Not only do algae thrive (see pages 55–6) but they use up all the oxygen leaving the water 'dead' for most plants and creatures. This is known as **hypertrophication**. (Stimulating plant growth is called **eutrophication**.) Longer disposal pipes merely disperse the sewage over a wider area. Dumping sewage solids at sea has been practised by cities such as New York and London. There is much evidence to show that dumped material from London finds its way back up river. One proposal is for the dumping of sewage sludge at great depths of about four km (two-and-a-half miles). The real answer is to recycle sewage as a soil fertilizer.

ABUSES – THE KILLING FIELDS

Most of the fish species we eat are collected from the sea using enormous nets or lines with baited hooks. Unfortunately creatures that are not wanted are caught along with those that are needed. For the ten or so prawns in every prawn cocktail, another 30 or more other creatures have been needlessly killed. Their unnecessary loss affects other marine life.

Of all the creatures which live in the oceans of the world, none has had more attention paid to it than the whale, of which there are many varieties. Why is this? Probably because:

- whales are so big
- whales take a long time to reproduce
- whalemeat is unnecessary as a food
- only a small part of the whale is used for food
- some whales are in danger of extinction
- killing methods are seen to be cruel.

A Greenpeace inflatable dinghy challenges a Japanese whaling ship in the Northern Ross Sea, in 1989.

The introduction of factory ships has meant that whaling can take place in remote areas such as the Antarctic Ocean. The hunter vessels are able to make quick return trips to the catching zones after leaving their previous catch with the 'mother' ship. Some whales have been hunted almost to extinction. As a result the International Whaling Commission (IWC) was formed in 1946 to try to control whaling. It has no legal way of enforcing its decisions but it has caused most countries to recognize the danger to whales and to stop whaling. Japan, Iceland and Norway have continued whaling on a much reduced scale under the pretext of 'scientific investigation'. In May 1991 the IWC met in Iceland to discuss a partial resumption of whaling in the Antarctic in 1992. A decision was deferred but Iceland may well leave the IWC as a result. At the time of writing a ban on whaling is still the official policy.

Drift netting

Modern drift nets are made of fine filament nylon. They are virtually invisible under the water. As fish cannot swim backwards, and the mesh of the net is small, any creatures hitting the net will be trapped. If it is a mammal like a seal, it will drown. In the Pacific, nets of up to 160 km (100 miles) in length are allowed to drift freely catching whatever is in their path. Each is a 'Wall of Death'. The result is the indiscriminate catching of fish and unwanted creatures. Even sea birds become entangled as they

Faroe Islanders have traditionally caught whales by driving them inshore and then slaughtering them in the water, so that the whole sea turns blood red. The occasion is a festival, with most of the islanders watching or taking part.

dive beneath the ocean surface for their food. A demand for a global ban on drift nets is growing, with a group of 15 nations in the South Pacific Forum taking the lead. Taiwan and Japan reluctantly agreed to cease using drift nets by the end of 1992. South Korea may soon follow after the United Nations also resolved to ban such nets.

Overfishing

The main reason for a decline in fish stocks has been overfishing. So many fish are taken from the sea that no breeding stock is left, with the result that whole species disappear from their normal

The results of overfishing

Anchovies off Peru
In 1971–72 the huge anchovy shoals virtually disappeared.
Haddock in the NW Atlantic
250,000 tonnes caught in 1965. 20,000 tonnes in 1974.
Herring in the North Sea
East coast fishing fleets caught four million tonnes annually before 1960 but only one million by 1970.
Capelin off Norway
Virtually none in 1987–88. Starving harp seals ruined nets as they tried to rob the very small catches.
Sardines off California
500,000 tonnes in the 1930s. Under 50,000 tonnes in 1950.
Chub mackerel in the Pacific and Atlantic
Japan took two million tonnes from the NW Pacific in 1978 but less than 500,000 tonnes in 1982.

habitats. One obvious improvement would be to increase the mesh size of nets so that small creatures could escape and young fish would be allowed to grow large enough to become breeding stock themselves. Quota systems which limit the amount fishing boats can catch are most effective but often seen as unfair by the fishing industry. European Community quotas make headline news in European papers with hostile reaction from the ports affected. The examples of overfishing on these pages indicate some of the problems of the past.

Death by drowning

The drowned dolphin floated onto the shore, its body partly eaten by crabs. More than enough was left to see that its body was scarred with a pattern which resembled the mesh of a net. Some strands of very fine nylon were entangled around its head. How did a creature so expert at swimming and so lithe in the water come to die from drowning? Despite its adaptation to the water the dolphin is a mammal like a horse, an elephant, a mouse, a whale or a person; prevent any of them breathing by keeping them under water and they will drown. Each, including the dolphin and the whale has to take in fresh air.

This particular dolphin was yet another victim of the 'Wall of Death'. The ocean slaughterhouse is mostly a response to our quest for certain fish and other marine creatures, usually for food. Much that is caught is not required, and like the beached dolphin, thrown back into the ocean. This is not only a waste, but it is an environmental disaster, as the balance of ocean life is upset. With some creatures the slaughter has led, or is leading, to their extinction: some whales and some turtles, for instance, have virtually disappeared altogether.

Something must be done. Some species have been saved but others are still at risk from peoples' deliberate or accidental actions. Even some attempts to manage the situation and at the same time meet the demand for the produce of the sea, has created other environmental hazards. Fish farming is one of these (see pages 28–9).

The sand eel is very common along most coasts of the North Atlantic. Many birds and fish feed on this lowly creature, but overfishing of sand eels for farm fertilizer has caused the disappearance of its predators.

Cans of tuna are shown as 'Dolphin Friendly' as the processor certifies that they have been caught without damage to dolphins.

NUTRITION
Sainsbury's tuna Chunks in Soya Oil are a good source of Niacin which helps food to give us energy

	TYPICAL VALUES OF DRAINED PRODUCT PER 100g (3½ oz)
ENERGY	160 k CALORIES 665 k JOULES
PROTEIN	279 g
CARBOHYDRATE	less than 0.1g
TOTAL FAT	
ADDED SALT	
VITAMINS	5.1g
	0.7g
NIACIN	% OF RECOMMENDED DAILY AMOUNT 60%

SAINSBURY'S TUNA IS CAUGHT WITH A POLE AND LINE (RATHER THAN BEING TRAWLED) THUS AVOIDING DANGER TO OTHER MARINE LIFE

SAINSBURY'S TUNA CHUNKS in soya oil
HIGH PROTEIN

DOLPHIN FRIENDLY

ABUSES – FROM THE AIR

Dumping directly into the sea is a source of pollution obvious to any onlooker. What is less obvious is the deposition of pollutants into the ocean from the air above. The emissions from chimneys and vehicle exhaust pipes; pesticides, herbicides and fertilizers which contaminate the air rather than contribute to farming; gases from rice paddy fields; flatulence from cattle and other domestic animals; chemical and gas leakages from industrial plants, oil rig, pipe line, coal mine and rubbish disposal; all these combine with the natural vapours from volcanoes, swamplands, grass and forest fires, and are blown by the wind across land and sea.

Take the North Sea for example. Factory chimneys and vehicle exhaust pipes of neighbouring countries propel solid waste airborne into the sea. These are the current estimates for one year:

Nitrogen compounds – 40,000 tonnes
Mercury 10 – 30 tonnes
Cadmium 45 – 240 tonnes
Lead 2,600 – 7,400 tonnes
Phosphorous compounds – 10,000 tonnes

Emitted gases (sulphur dioxide, nitrogen oxides and carbon dioxide) produce acid rain which also falls onto the ocean. This may have little effect on the overall average acidity of sea water (about 8.3 pH, which is alkaline and not acid) but in sensitive areas around the coasts, where over 90 per cent of all marine life is to be found, it adds to the acidic surge of springtime input from the rivers.

The lipid microlayer, (the top few millimetres of the ocean), receives the bulk of this airborne 'invasion'. The high level of nitrogen entering the ocean from the air adds to the destructive effects of sewage by stimulating the growth of algae.

Incineration at sea

Some of the most toxic of chemicals have been, in the past, loaded onto special incineration ships and taken out to sea. When sufficiently far from the shore the chemicals were burnt at temperatures high enough, so it was claimed, to destroy 99.9 per cent of the poisons – providing everything was working properly. In 1991 two ships were still operating in the North Sea and were said to burn about 90,000 tonnes of chemicals annually. Only 0.1 per cent unburnt may not sound very much, but this means out of the 90,000 tonnes at least **90 tonnes of the most toxic of chemicals** fell from the exhaust fumes. These poisons do not rot away in the water but remain to accumulate in the bodies of marine life, as with the poisons dumped directly into the sea. There is great opposition to ocean incineration; it has been banned in the Baltic and Mediterranean Seas and in the ocean areas under the control of

By 1994, the practice of burning the most noxious chemicals at sea will have finished. Until then, and afterwards with 'ordinary wastes', pollution of the ocean will result from the exhaust fumes spreading from the chimneys of the incinerator ships.

the USA. The North Sea Conference, in 1987, agreed to reduce the burning of waste at sea by 65 per cent by 1991 and to ban it completely by the end of 1994. One extra problem is that the burning of some chemicals actually produces deadly poisonous **dioxins**. The London Dumping Conference banned the burning of noxious liquid chemicals at sea worldwide from 1994 – but the burning of rubbish and oil waste can continue.

The Greenhouse Effect

Without the atmospheric gases of the earth's atmosphere retaining heat, our planet would be as cold as Venus. But the burning of fossil fuel from industry and power stations over the past 100 years has increased the amount of CO_2

Carbon dioxide disposal in the oceans

It has been suggested by a Cambridge University scientist named Raymond Harrowell that the output of CO_2 from the world's oil- and coal-fired power stations could be piped out to sea to be absorbed by the water between seven and thirty metres below the surface. According to Harrowell, after 100 years the output of CO_2 from 10,000 two mega-watt power stations would have saturated only 0.04 per cent of the oceans. The theory may be correct but could it be done in practice? It would provide a solution to the global Greenhouse Effect of extra CO_2 from electricity generation if Harrowell's idea could be made to work.

and other gases to such an extent that the temperature of the atmosphere is rising. By 2050 AD it will be one to four-and-a-half degrees centigrade higher than now. The ocean beneath it will warm too, but at a slower rate. As a result the level of the sea will rise as warm water expands to occupy more space and the Antarctic ice melts to release more water. Any appreciable rise in sea level will flood the land, deposit salt on the soil and cause a considerable movement of coastal population further inland. Those countries liable to be flooded without the necessary finance to improve sea defences, Bangladesh for example, will find it impossible to cope unless richer nations decide to offer help.

Even now the flooding of the majestic piazza of Venice is not uncommon. It is becoming more usual and much concern is felt for the safety of the whole of Venice as sea levels rise.

Global warming of only a few degrees may make the difference between the wet monsoon of Asia operating 'normally' or failing to materialize. The critical temperature seems to be 28°C. Above this, the moisture-laden air stays trapped over the ocean. Since the whole of the agriculture of the monsoon lands relies on the rain of the wet monsoon, any failure – as sometimes happens now – would be disastrous and would result in famine conditions.

On the bright side, many scientists believe that the extremes of sea level rise are much exaggerated. The best policy must be to reduce the emission of greenhouse gases into the air and thus to slow down global warming.

The ozone layer

Chlorofluorocarbon (CFC) gases destroy the ozone layer, where at great height above the earth, the ozone filters out harmful ultraviolet rays. The UVB rays destroy

plankton leading to less food for creatures which feed on it and less CO_2 absorption by the phytoplankton (see pages 19–20).

Into the air

The movement is not all from air to sea: gases from the sea also move into the air, contributing to environmental problems:

- chlorine gas rises from the ocean surface
- the sea provides single atoms of oxygen which combine with atmospheric oxygen to form ozone, which is harmful to people at ground level
- some algae emit sulphur products which contribute to acid rain formation

ABUSES – THE INLAND SEAS

The one feature which characterizes all inland seas is that the outward flow of water is limited. This means that any pollution poured into them will tend to build up rather than disperse into the vast breadth and depth of the oceans. Those inland waters surrounded by heavily populated and industrial areas are at greatest risk from continually rising pollution levels. Such pollution will not only create direct hazards to health and welfare but will poison the fish and shellfish exploited for food.

Extra nitrate from agricultural excess and sewage disposal will stimulate the growth of algae so as to despoil the shore and deoxygenate the water until nothing but the lowest form of marine life can survive. The situation is worst where major rivers empty into the sea after they have travelled through several countries which, though far removed from the sea, use the river as a convenient waste disposal channel for their industrial effluent.

In Venice, workmen remove 800 tonnes of seaweed every day.

The shrinking seas

Landlocked inland seas depend for their existence on the supply of water from their catchment rivers. These same rivers will flow through lands where water is needed for agriculture and drinking. Irrigation schemes and dams will store or divert the water until the seas shrink as they are 'starved' of their normal input. If such human-made conditions combine with an extended period of natural drought, the future prospects for the inland seas will be bleak.

It is probably true to say that all inland seas and large lakes are having problems of one sort or another connected with the environment. The most publicized is the Mediterranean Sea with its own internal areas such as the Adriatic and Aegean Seas – inland seas within an inland sea, as it were. There are few problems of inland sea abuse which are not found in the Mediterranean.

Venice

Venice is world famous for its unique location, with its buildings lapped by the waters of canal and lagoon linked directly to the Adriatic. From the air, ugly blotches can be seen on the lagoon surface. Venice, often described as the most beautiful city on earth, is besieged by algae. The main one is a large species of seaweed known as *ulva rigida*. Within the lagoon it is producing about 30,000 tonnes a year. It is fed by the nitrates from the fertilizers applied to the crops of the Po valley, whose river estuary lies south of Venice. The tonnes of sewage discharged into the lagoon and surrounding coastal areas from the resident population and the millions of tourists also provide abundant food for the algae. Phosphates in the detergents used in home and hotel also stimulate growth. What can be done with all this seaweed? Drying it and using it as organic fertilizer would be the ideal solution, but it is a difficult and expensive process. Should we dump it and let it rot? This would lead to plagues of mosquitoes and other insects. In 1986 the flies were so bad that planes could not land at Marco Polo Airport (Venice) because they would have skidded out of control on squashed bodies. The smell of rotting seaweed is obnoxious, and the sulphurous fumes given off create acid rain.

Then there is the foaming mass of red, yellow, green and brown jelly-like algae which affects the whole coastline from Venice southwards. It, too, attracts insects and although it is not poisonous, it is unpleasant for those trying to enjoy a seaside holiday. During July 1990 the mayors of ten Adriatic resorts brought buckets full of the algae to the square in front of the Italian Parliament in Rome and staged a protest 'sit-in'.

Mestre, the industrial city beside Venice, used to discharge its toxic effluent into the lagoon. Now pollution controls have stopped this, the irony being that at one time these chemicals effectively killed off most of the algae.

The Mediterranean is considered to be one of the most oil-fouled areas of water in the world. Some half to one million tonnes of oil are estimated to be discharged into the 'Med' annually, mainly from the large number of merchant ships and tankers using it. Happily the general problem has been reduced by better oil waste handling facilities in Mediterranean ports. The Persian Gulf, another area of water which can be considered an inland sea, has suffered a great deal from oil pollution, both accidental and deliberate (see page 41).

The bays and inlets around both the east and west coasts of the USA, suffer from so much pollution that the term 'black mayonnaise' has been given to the thick layers of toxic sludge blanketing parts of the shores and coastal waters – it is especially vile in Boston Harbour in the east and Puget Sound, beside Seattle, in the west.

The annual input of *some* pollutants entering the Mediterranean from the surrounding land (in tonnes):

Pollutant	Quantity
organic matter	12 million
phosphorous	320,000
nitrogen	800,000
mercury	100
lead	3,800
chromium	2,400
zinc	21,000
phenols	12,000
detergents	60,000
chlorine-based pesticides	90

Source World Health Organization.

The Aral Sea

The Aral Sea, in the former USSR, used to be about the size of Ireland. It is one of the inland seas affected by the diversion of irrigation water from its two main contributory rivers. The Aral, the fourth largest inland sea in the world, has shrunk by a third since the 1950s and threatens the whole region with ecological disaster. The original shore is now 100 km (60 miles) from the water's edge, and the water itself has become too salty for fish and too shallow for even moderately sized ships. Strict measures were introduced in the late 1980s to control irrigation losses, as a result of which, large quantities of water have been saved to replenish the sea.

The abandoned ship below bears testimony to the fact that the Aral Sea has shrunk.

The map shows how the Aral Sea has shrunk between 1960 and 1990.

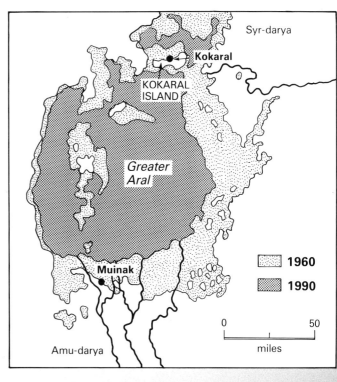

WHAT'S TO BE DONE?

The European Community bathing water quality scheme, allows a blue flag to be raised at beaches where the water is of adequate quality for safe bathing. Water is tested weekly.

The use of land in developed countries is strictly controlled by planning laws and procedures, and the boundaries between countries are clearly defined. Generally, what 'belongs' to whom is known to all and border controls restrict movement and enforce the national laws. Although the immediate coasts and sea areas of countries are also under national control, the majority of the ocean lacks specific controls. The traditional 'freedom of the high seas' has been questioned and attempts to reach international agreement at recent conferences have involved not only the rights of access to coastal waters, but also the control of fishing grounds and the exploitation of sea-bed mineral resources. The control of the ocean is still a vexed question and much international discussion will be needed to bring some semblance of order to the water world.

UNCLOS

On 30 April 1982, the United Nations Conference on the Law of the Sea (UNCLOS) voted to adopt the Convention on the Law of the Sea. The Convention not only deals with the international areas of the oceans but also provides important rules for the control of the seas by coastal states. The Convention comes into force when it has been agreed by 60 states; by 1990, 44 had done so. The longest part of the convention deals with the future exploration and exploitation of the ocean bottom in areas beyond the continental shelf. There would be an International Sea-Bed Authority which would be authorized to conduct its own mining operations through an organization called Enterprise. The resources of the ocean bed would be managed, in the words of the document, as a 'common heritage of mankind'.

The 'Regional Seas' of the UN Environment Programme

Arabian Gulf
Caribbean
East Africa
East Asia
Mediterranean
Red Sea/Gulf of Aden
South Asia
South Pacific
West and Central Africa

Basically UNCLOS sets the rules for control of the ocean areas nearest to the land. It goes on to oblige states to use 'the best practical means at their disposal' to prevent and control marine pollution from any source. They would be bound to cooperate globally and regionally to raise standards of environmental protection of the oceans. As far as ocean research is concerned, coastal states would control what went on in their own off-shore areas, but would be obliged to permit other countries to carry out their own peaceful research as necessary. States would be expected to develop marine technology (deep-sea diving methods for example) and to make it available to other states on fair and reasonable terms and conditions.

Is it happening?

Up to the beginning of 1991, the United Nations Environment Programme (UNEP) had established ten Regional Seas with the backing of 120 countries. Of these Regional Seas Action Plans

Although individual people can do many things to help keep the oceans in a healthy state, the major matters have to be put right at international level, with meetings such as this one at the United Nations in New York.

(RSAP), that of the Mediterranean Sea has been the most successful. Of the others, only those of the Caribbean, Arabian Gulf and the South Pacific have made much progress. Basically the RSAPs believe that global oceanic pollution will be slowed only by cooperative programmes at regional levels, and that the problems of the oceans result from misuse of the land. The UN Ocean and Coastal Programme Activity Centre maintains a watch on ocean problems.

'The New Ocean Regime' has recently been introduced by UNCLOS, so, with the UNEP programme, something has at last begun to be done about the 'health' of the oceans. The question 'What's to be done?' is, therefore, partially answered by the hope that countries all over the world will cooperate one with the other. This will be most effective when a few countries in each area get together to resolve their local problem. For

Logo of the UN Conference on the Law Of the Sea (UNCLOS).

Example of a regional agreement

NASCO (see page 48), which sets the quotas for North Atlantic salmon netting, has allowed the Faroes to sell their rights to a catch of 550 tonnes to a Canadian, American and British group of angling organizations. This will mean that the larger salmon will be left to return to their spawning rivers where the anglers will have 'better' sport. The question is, when will Britain ban drift-net fishing for salmon off the north east English coast as it already has off the Scottish coast?

example, the Baltic countries such as Sweden and Finland, have an interest in the Baltic Sea. The European Community states are specially concerned with the North Sea and the effects of pollution on the beaches of the seaside resorts. Britain and Eire must pay attention to the Irish Sea, and the countries around the Mediterranean must continue to cooperate on matters of pollution control in that area. In the Pacific the states of the southern area have restricted the use of drift netting.

It is difficult to enforce rules and regulations on a world-wide scale. It is certainly easier to do it in more restricted regional areas where governments close to one another cooperate, for example, the USA and Canada. Otherwise it is sometimes necessary for influential nations to apply econ-

omic sanctions against those countries who break the agreed code of practice. Denying Japan the right to export fish products to the USA may well act as an influence on restricting Japanese whaling activities.

As individuals, it is unrealistic to expect each of us to be able to alter the conduct of nations that overfish the seas, or large industries that pollute the seas. But it is possible to support campaigns which aim to remedy particular problems. For example, if we buy only 'dolphin-friendly' tuna (see page 49), other packers will be forced to take similar action if they are to remain in business. Those of us who live fairly near to the sea should discover how local sewage disposal takes place. Is the effluent properly treated or is it merely discharged straight into the sea? If the disposal method is unsatisfactory it is up to us to support those politicians who are prepared to alter the situation.

Perhaps the most important thing that we, as individuals, can do is to take an interest in the oceans and to realize that we cannot go on abusing them as we do now. The well-being of the ocean is directly linked to the future well-being of the world.

Of all things to bring benefit to the oceans would be the introduction by all nations of the **Precautionary principle**.
This means that nothing would be discharged into the sea unless it had been proved scientifically **not** to harm the environment.

GLOSSARY

Aquaculture
Farming in water.

Bloom
High concentration of plankton.

Buoy
Floating object to aid navigation of ships.

Coral reef
Rock in tropical water formed by the coral polyp.

Dredge
Collecting sediment from the river or sea-bed.

Estuary
Where a river joins the sea.

European Community (EC)
The affiliation of 12 European countries including the UK. Also known as The Common Market, with headquarters in Brussels.

Factory ship
Large ship to which fishing boats take their catch of fish to be processed.

Greenpeace
Organization that tries to prevent environmental damage.

Habitat
Natural home of a plant or animal.

Ice Cap
The ice covering at the two poles, Arctic (North), Antarctic (South).

Knot
Measurement of speed on water. One knot is one nautical mile per hour.

Longshore drift
Movement of pebbles, sand etc, along the shore by the waves.

Mangrove
Tree which grows on tropical shores of rivers and seas.

Photosynthesis
Process by which plants use sunlight to make food.

Plankton
Small plants (phytoplankton) and animals (zooplankton) which live in the top part of the sea.

Radar
System of navigation which relies on an electrical impulse bouncing back to be displayed on a TV screen.

Sewage (raw)
Human waste usually flushed away down a toilet.

Sewage sludge
Solid waste that settles out of raw sewage by gravity.
(raw) Untreated sewage sludge.
(digested) Sludge that has been fermented until it decomposes.
(activated) Digested sludge which has had a second fermentation and is then dried.

Submersible
Underwater vessel in which the crew is kept at normal air pressure.

UNCLOS
United Nations Conference on the Law Of the Sea.

UNEP
United Nations Environment Programme.

RESOURCES AND ADDRESSES

Magazines

The Courier, February 1986, UNESCO
National Geographic, Volume 160, No 6 December 1981
Nature and Resources, Volume 26, No 2 1990, UNESCO

Books

Atlas of the Sea around the British Isles, Ministry of Agriculture, Fisheries and Food, 1981
Conservation 2000 Series, Batsford:
  The Greenhouse Effect, Philip Neal 1992
  The Ozone Layer, Philip Neal 1993
Considering Conservation Series, Dryad Press:
  Energy, Power Sources and Electricity, Philip Neal 1989
  The Greenhouse Effect and Ozone Layer, Philip Neal 1989
  Hunting, Shooting and Fishing, Philip Neal 1987
  War on Waste, Joy Palmer 1988
  The World's Water, Joy Palmer 1987
The Cousteau Almanac, Jacques-Yves Cousteau, Columbus Books 1981
Dictionary of Environment and Development, Andy Crump, Earthscan 1991
A Dictionary of the Environment, Steve Elsworth, Paladin 1990
The Gaia Atlas of Planet Management, Norman Myers, Pan Books 1985
Harvest from the Sea, Oxfam, 1985 (Posters and teaching set)
The Oceans, David Lambert, Ward Lock 1979
Oceans and Seas, T. Jennings, Oxford University Press 1988
The Ocean World of Jacques Cousteau, Ed. Richard Murphy, Angus & Robertson (UK) 1975

Our Common Seas, Don Hinrichsen, Earthscan 1990
Restless Oceans (Planet Earth Series), A.B.C. Whipple, Time Life

Useful addresses

Dept of Agriculture, Fisheries and Food for Scotland
Marine Laboratory
P O Box 101
Victoria Road
Aberdeen AB9 8DB

English Nature
Northminster House
Peterborough
Cambridgeshire PE1 1UA

Friends of the Earth (UK)
26–28 Underwood Street
London N1 7JQ

Friends of the Earth (USA)
218 D Street South East
Washington D C 20003
USA

Greenpeace (UK)
Canonbury Villas
London N1 2PN

Greenpeace (USA)
1436 U Street North West
Washington D C 20009
USA

Marine Conservation Society
4 Gloucester Road
Ross-on-Wye
Herefordshire HR9 5BU

Marine Information & Advisory Service
Deacon Laboratory
Brook Road
Wormley
Godalming GU8 5UB

Ministry of Agriculture, Fisheries and Food
Whitehall Place
London SW1A 1HB

Nuclear Industry Radioactive Waste Executive (NIREX)
Curie Avenue
Harwell
Didcot OX11 ORA

Royal National Lifeboat Institution
West Quay Road
Poole
Dorset BH15 1HZ

Seafish Industry Authority
Seafish House
St Andrew's Dock
Hull HU3 4QE
  and
HQ – 10 Young Street
Edinburgh EH2 4JQ

Shellfish Association of Great Britain
Fishmongers' Hall
London Bridge
London EC4R 9EL

UK Atomic Energy Authority
11 Charles II Street
London SW1Y 4QP

United Nations Environment Programme (UNEP)
P O Box 30552
Nairobi
Kenya
East Africa

World Wide Fund for Nature (UK)
Panda House
Weyside Park
Godalming
Surrey GU7 1XR

World Wide Fund for Nature (USA)
1250 24th Street North West
Washington D C 20037
USA

INDEX